Cedar Mesa

Gregory McNamee, SERIES EDITOR

Cedar Mesa

A Place Where Spirits Dwell

TEXT BY David Petersen

PHOTOGRAPHS BY Branson Reynolds

The University of Arizona Press   Tucson

The University of Arizona Press
© 2002 David Petersen
First Printing
All rights reserved

07 06 05 04 03 02   6 5 4 3 2 1

Library of Congress Cataloging-in-Publication Data appear on the last printed
page of this book.

British Library Cataloguing-in-Publication Data
A catalogue record for this book is available from the British Library.

Frontispiece: Owachomo Natural Bridge, Natural Bridges National Monument

This book is dedicated to the memory of

CACTUS ED ABBEY

and to all of those who, through their own brave words and deeds,
keep his spirit alive.

contents

CONTENTS

X

photographs

PHOTOGRAPHS

xii

acknowledgments

My longtime friend and partner in this (ad)venture is Durango photographer Branson Reynolds, who knows Cedar Mesa as a lover knows his love. Even as I scribble these thoughts in the comfort of my little writing shack (my wife calls it the Outhouse, though I can't imagine why), Branson has embarked on yet another solo venture there, four hours' drive west of our neighboring mountain cabins, stalking the visible spirit of the place, cameras in hand, on behalf of this joint effort. It was Branson who first introduced me to Cedar Mesa's once-foreign, vaguely forbidding moonscape of sky, space, stone, and sun. Even today, twenty years of independent exploration later,

Branson continues to expand my understanding and love of this inimitable island of sand and sandstone, mesa and canyon, past and present conjoined. And so it is that not only Branson's photographs but also his gentle, charismatic character invest and illuminate the stories to come.

Another Cedar Mesa mentor and recurring character in these pages is my late friend and teacher "Cactus Ed" Abbey. If you've not read Abbey but love wild country and the personal freedom and dignity natural wildness fosters and preserves, give yourself a gift and read Abbey's classic canyon-country memoir *Desert Solitaire*. Then read his rowdy eco-adventure novel *The Monkey Wrench Gang*, a comedy of hope set on and around Cedar Mesa. In company with the ghosts of Anasazi Indians and rough-riding cowboys, Abbey's anarchic spirit happily haunts this rock-desert place—then, now, forever.

Portions of this book are adapted from my essay collection *The Nearby Faraway: A Personal Journey through the Heart of the West*, and appear here thanks to Stephen Topping and the other good folk at Johnson Books of Boulder, Colorado.

Finally, for inviting my participation in this project, and for his patient shepherding throughout, I am grateful to Desert Places series editor Gregory McNamee.

Very well. Travel light, go slow, watch your every step, and don't get caught out after dark. In fact, in the spirit of Abbey, try not to get caught at all. Good luck to us, then, every one.

—D.P.
from the Outhouse
San Juan Mountains, Colorado

glossary of canyon country terms

(Read me first!)

Hoodoos: Sandstone formations, most often vertical columns, eroded to resemble people, animals, and all manner of spooky beings.

Mesa/mesa: Spanish for table top. A broad expanse of high, mostly flat, sparsely timbered land. Many smaller mesas (lower-case) combine to form *the* Mesa (capitalized).

Microbiotic crust: A delicate, slow-growing, crusty, living skin of lichen that forms atop the sand, aiding water retention while slowing wind erosion. In older texts, this same canyon-country phenomenon is called cryptogamic soil.

Slickrock: Any large expanse of weathered sandstone, often weirdly eroded: smooth compared to jagged, but in no way slick.

Tinaja: Pronounced tin-AH-ha, Spanish for tank, or pool. A natural depression or pothole in the slickrock that forms a catchbasin for rainwater and snowmelt; some tinajas are as large as small swimming pools.

Cedar Mesa

introduction

It has been proposed that North America has lost all of its sacred places to "progress," and that most Americans wouldn't recognize the sacred in nature if it slapped them in the face.

For most of America and most Americans, both of these proposals are sadly true. Yet, for those fortunate few who know where and, more important, *how* to search for and discern the sacred in nature, it damn well still exists. And nowhere in North America are such enclaves of natural landscape magic more plentiful and evident than right here in the American West, my home: the mountains, the seashore, the deserts.

Within this enchanted realm, Cedar Mesa, in southeast Utah,

is a uniquely magical desert place. Elevation varies wildly but averages 6,000 feet. It is sandy mesas and slickrock escarpments. It is deep-blue skies and dark-green mountains far away. It is an elegant maze of vertical-walled, vertigo-inspiring canyons plunging to darkened depths, animated by towering, lifelike hoodoos. Ironically, there are no cedars on Cedar Mesa. The term is a tenacious regional misnomer for the ubiquitous Utah juniper *(Juniperus osteoperma),* whose core wood when split, and incense aroma when burned, are strikingly cedarlike, yet not.

While you can see it as fleeting shadows, smell it in the morning air and evening wood smoke, sense it in the very pores of your sun-parched skin, the ultimate essence that renders Cedar Mesa such a distinctly surreal place and experience remains tauntingly beyond comprehension, a tantalizing mystery, waiting always just around the next bend in the canyon walls, just beyond sensory reach. Here lurks an ethereal *power*, an otherworldly feeling that defies description yet is palpable as you descend into the slickrock canyons and hike the gritty mesas—beneath the vaulting sky, through the profound silence, breathing deep the sweet clean air that grants and unites all life. This is a place frozen in time; a time frozen in place; a rolling sea of rock-hard waves: desert-hot in summer, cold as snow in winter.

Unlike the American desert of the popular imagination, Cedar Mesa is no saguaro-studded cowboy movie set. While smaller cacti—most commonly prickly pear, claret-cup, fish-hook, and hedgehog—bless the Mesa with dazzling color during their brief flowering seasons, this is not cactus, but "P-J" country—local lingo for the piñon-pine/juniper "pygmy forest" ecology. Sage-

Evening primrose on Cedar Mesa

brush, as well, thrives in the sandy soil of the mesas. The precious few perennial watering places to be found here, almost always down in the canyons, often reveal themselves from afar by the groves of age-gnarled Fremont cottonwoods that fringe and shade them—the trees drinking deeply through their roots, yet slowing evaporation with their lush and shimmering summer foliage.

Each in its own time, desert-adapted wildflowers—Indian paintbrush, scarlet gilia, globe mallow, sand verbena, sego lily (the Utah state flower), cliffrose, sacred datura, evening primrose, yucca, monkey flower, rabbitbrush, sunflower, vetch, prince's plume, columbine, and dozens more—electrify this "barren" landscape with a spectrum and brilliance of hues to shame any rainbow.

In addition to its biological splendor, Cedar Mesa—situated as it is near the heart of the tremendous Colorado Plateau (which, in turn, straddles the legendary Four Corners region where Arizona, Colorado, New Mexico, and Utah meet)—encompasses magnificent examples of all the essential topographic and geologic wonders that define "canyon country" throughout the American Southwest, including stone arches, windows, hoodoos, the world's most impressive display of natural bridges, breath-sucking precipices, hidden springs, hanging gardens, moss-fringed pools, and a treasure of pre-Columbian Indian ruins.

Adding significantly to the glory of what Cedar Mesa *is*, is what Cedar Mesa *is not*—not nearly so on-the-beaten-path, commercially hyped, and woefully overdeveloped as its better-known

Anasazi ruin in Mule Canyon

neighbors, Canyonlands and Arches national parks, two hours' drive to the north, bracketing the tiny uranium mining-cum-tourist boomtown of Moab. Happily for those of us who know, love, and wish to protect the place from such ruinous "progress," you won't even find Cedar Mesa named on most road maps.

This sprawling expanse of purely public land is managed (for better and worse) primarily by the BLM (Bureau of Land Management—or, as its critics interpret the acronym, "Bureau of Livestock Minions"). While much of the Mesa currently enjoys Wilderness Study Area protection, that doesn't stop the cows or the ATV (all-terrain vehicle) cowboys, and the designation remains vulnerable to political whim. While largely unspoiled today, Cedar Mesa has taken some hard licks with plenty more in store.

Regarding boundaries: Apropos to such a rugged landscape, Cedar Mesa means different things to different people. On a topographical map, the Mesa is demarked to the east by the toothy upthrust of Comb Ridge, boldly inscribing a north-south line. On road maps, Comb Ridge is rarely shown, so search the southeast corner of Utah for U.S. Highway 191, a curvaceous north-south two-lane connecting the Mormon pioneer villages of Blanding and Bluff. Comb Ridge runs parallel to U.S. 191, a few miles west.

Moving clockwise from Bluff, the Mesa's southern limit is easier to trace, as the land drops abruptly away, plunging hundreds of feet to mostly pancake sand-and-sage desert, following a jagged line crudely traced by U.S. 163 between Bluff and the riverside village of Mexican Hat. However, most veteran

Goosenecks of the San Juan River

Mesaheads extend its southern border for aesthetic reasons a few miles beyond the drop, to the north bank of the serpentine San Juan River, beyond which sprawls the Navajo Indian Reservation. With this modest addition in miles come some strikingly immodest extras, including especially Mexican Hat rock (one of nature's most awesome and unlikely balancing acts); Valley of the Gods (a tower-, spire-, and hoodoo-studded sister to nearby Monument Valley); and Goosenecks (of the San Juan River) State Park and overlook.

Turning north from U.S. 163 onto Utah 261, we low-gear up the unpaved (except on exceptionally dangerous curves), adrenaline-pumping (especially on those same white-knuckle curves) Moki Dugway. *Moki*, with various spellings, is a local term for the ancient Anasazi Indians, while a dugway is a steep, switchbacking road or trail carved, or dug, into a cliff side—basically, a glorified mountain-goat trail.

At the top of Moki Dugway the pavement resumes—though soon a sandy side road doglegs four miles west, to Muley Point overlook. It was on this windy aerie, in the late 1980s, that photographer Branson Reynolds and I almost froze to death one deep-below-zero December night when our skimpy backpack tent was assaulted by a surprise blizzard. And even then, at the worst of times, the place was stunningly beautiful, offering as it does a vulture's-eye view of Monument Valley in the distance, John's Canyon directly below, and segments of the San Juan River, far, far below and away. If the season is warm and rain has recently fallen, the many tinajas dotting Muley Point pulse with squirming, tenacious life: water boatmen, whirligig beetles,

Edge of Cedar Mesa at Muley Point

backswimmers, water striders, snails, fairy shrimp, and at the pinnacle of the pothole hierarchy, spadefoot toads.

Back on the pavement and continuing north, undulant little Utah 261 fairly splits Cedar Mesa up its belly (which is to say, you cannot drive the Mesa's western edge), with the roadless, ruins-rich Grand Gulch Primitive Area spreading to the sunset horizon. As it should be with all truly primitive places, the surreal essence of this priceless natural and cultural preserve, Grand Gulch, remains wholly invisible from the highway. To experience Grand Gulch for the hidden treasure it is, you must abandon your wheels and explore its hundred twisting miles of trail by boot or saddle. The ringing *quiet* you'll meet down there alone justifies the effort.

To complete this superficial windshield circumnavigation of Cedar Mesa, take Utah Highway 95 east from its junction with state 261, roller-coasting back toward U.S. 191, which you'll rejoin just below Blanding.

With that necessary bit of journalistic orienting said, done, and notwithstanding, be it known that this is not yet another hand-holding, give-it-all-away, chamber-of-commerce style guidebook, of which there are far too many already, far too often superficially researched, impersonally written, and shamelessly detailed in pursuit of paltry profit at the expense of natural wildness, personal exploration, and true adventure.

To the contrary precisely, this little tome, like its kin in the Desert Places series, is intended to honor, celebrate, and in whatever measure possible help to protect one of the most palpably spiritual natural places remaining on the American continent—not to lay it open to accelerated ruin by encouraging recreational overuse and (since it invariably follows, like a trailing odor) commercial exploitation. Thus, while I'll not withhold place names and other details regarding specific locales and attractions already well known, much visited, and sufficiently protected, more sensitive secrets shall remain just that—secrets. It's a tricky bit of business in that while I wish to *acquaint* you with the area, to *intrigue* you with a true and intimate taste of its cloaked as well as its visible qualities, to help you *feel* its silent preternatural ambiance—and, perchance, to recruit your support for its enhanced and prolonged preservation—there has to be a limit. For your sake as well as mine and Cedar Mesa's, I can only trust that if you knew and felt about this place as I do, you would do the same.

Cedar Mesa, with its creased and crenulated topography and blessed sparsity of intrusive roads, designated and "improved" campgrounds, and maintained trails, is an Eden for personal (as opposed to guidebook) discovery—spiritual as well as geographical, interior as well as exterior—and hands-on adventure . . . including as much or little raw physical danger as you choose to accept. And along that winding path to who-knows-where-and-what, accessible only by foot and courageous will, is where nature's true magic invariably resides, patient as time itself. In the end, no guide, no guidebook, can take you there. You must seek and find it on your own.

PART I Up on the Mesa

a place where spirits dwell

Across two fortunate decades now, I've been exploring Cedar Mesa, spring and fall, when the weather is most inviting, often in the company of friends but more often, like now, joyously alone.

Abandoning my four-by-four pickup in the afternoon shade of a big piñon pine back on the two-track linear sand trap that passes for a road here in the midst of Cedar Mesa (and plenty good enough for me), I hiked the final way in. Now here I stand in awe, my bare uncertain toes gripping the cool gritty edge of a nameless sandstone gash tumbling a thousand feet down, down, into the black unknown. Down there in the narrow void, I note, it's already midnight.

Soon, feeling and fearing the magnetic pull of the shadowy abyss, I retreat in the fading twilight to my spartan camp, set unobtrusively at the edge of the twisted P-J forest. After dinner, as I sit sipping whisky and smoking a filthy cigarette and gazing into a sparking fire of fragrant piñon, listening to the sounds of an unabashedly natural night, it occurs to me that to unaccustomed eyes the rocky, glaring, semi-arid landscape of Cedar Mesa and the surrounding Colorado Plateau must seem desolate, foreboding, more dead than alive.

Not true.

Visible to anyone who really *looks* — which implies a patient and thoughtful alertness — are a wealth of diurnal creatures. Each morning and evening here, the turquoise sky swarms with feathered life: darting cliff swallows, bell-voiced canyon wrens, swifts graceful in aerobatic flight, hawks, falcons, eagles, vultures, blue-black iridescent ravens.

Meanwhile, down here on the ground, the deep cooling shade of piñon, juniper, and sage hides deer, rabbits, ground squirrels, lizards, snakes, the stodgy desert tortoise, and myriad species more. Including me.

And come the soothing darkness you need only listen in order to sense the abundance and exuberance of the local nightlife. Even now, as I sit here fireside and muse, a great-horned owl's repetitive query animates the moonless night. In time, the hooter's persistent plea — *Who, who is there?* — is answered by a melancholy nightjar: *Poor Will, Poor Will.* Perhaps stirred to action by the spooky threat of the nearby owl, some small, unseen rodent scurries among the sagebrush beyond the little fire's

Mule deer

flickering cave of light. And always—above, around, and through all other sounds—rings a cacophony of crickets.

In due time, mellow from my drink and the incensed piñon smoke, growing drowsy, I let the fire burn to coals, unfurl my nylon bag on the warm soft sand, and embrace the "little death" of sleep. No tent, and no need for one. Out here on the mesa, on a sublime spring night such as this, the low-roofed starry heavens are shelter plenty enough. Content beyond description, utterly untroubled by the troubling world outside, I drift gently away.

Waking to a morning made for exploration, I strap on a daypack and strike off south, bobbing across an undulating expanse of erosion-sculpted slickrock like petrified ocean swells. In fact and long ago, a shallow sea inundated most all of what is now the Colorado Plateau, its sandy shoreline ripples preserved for all eternity in this sandstone monument to time.

My morning's destination, a couple of miles away, is a long-abandoned Anasazi cliff dwelling clinging precariously to a narrow ledge beneath a shallow alcove overlooking a sandy flat some five hundred feet below. Virtually invisible from any angle or distance, to find the place you have to know it's there. A long time ago, friend Branson revealed it to me—a precious gift. Keeping the faith, I've shared it with scant few others, since a secret too-much revealed loses all its magic.

A lazy hour and more along, at the promontory above the alcove, I lower myself through a narrow cleft in the rimrock, skid and slide down a steep talus slope, and ease across the treacherous face of a slickrock expanse to a narrow ledge a hundred feet below. Hugging the exposed ledge across a vertical cliff face, trying not to look down, I emerge all weak and shaky at the entrance to the shallow rock shelter—a place where spirits dwell.

Three hundred years before Columbus—that famous first emissary for all land-grabbers to come—set sail, an extended family, or clan, of perhaps six or eight stone-age native farmers called this west-facing high-rise home. Today, the neighboring Navajo call those old ones *Anasazi*, meaning "ancient strangers," or "ancient enemies," depending on interpretation. Although agency anthropologists and others swayed by the current rage for nominal political correctness are attempting to substitute the demystifying and sterile term "pre-Puebloans," the old favorite term Anasazi, like "cedar," lives stoically on. And I for one openly endorse it.

In addition to dry-land farming and building sturdy dwellings of hand-shaped sandstone blocks cemented and faced with adobe (a mixture of mud, small stones, and grass), the Anasazi hunted, gathered wild plant foods, and fired finely painted pottery, black on white. Offering mute evidence of their skill and productivity as potters, palm-sized shards of mugs, jugs, bowls, and ladles lie strewn about the alcove floor. I pick up a few pieces and admire their imaginative geometric designs; like snowflakes, no two are precisely alike. Most remain clean and sharp, refuting eight plodding centuries of wind, rain, and roaring summer sun. One at a time, I return these broken shards of human history to their rightful places—not in some natty museum pile atop a rock, as children and childlike adults are wont to do at

Anasazi potsherds

more accessible ruins, but scattered as I found them, like memories in the powdered dust.

Amazingly, a few desiccated corncobs also survive, dehydrated and shrunken by the arid climate. These are the produce of a crop grown and harvested even as Kublai Khan and his Mongol mobs ran amok through Asia, even as a dreary Europe suffered through the unthinkable horrors of its morbid Middle Ages.

But were things so much better *here*, back then? What might have prompted these enigmatic people to nest on such risky aeries as this and thousands of similar others all across the Four Corners region of the American Southwest? The daily drudgery of hauling in food, water, and firewood along that hellish entrance ledge would have been not just labor-intensive, but life-threatening. And with only a few yards of sloping rock between your tiny stone sleeping shelter and the cliff's sharp edge, you could never allow your children out of sight, or hand, even for a moment. Not, at least, if you liked them.

So why *did* these clever irrigators, these gentle-seeming growers of corn, beans, and squash, these hunters and gatherers of wild foods, become cliff-side hermits?

A strong clue in this instance (as in so many similar others) is the tumbledown defensive wall erected across the narrowest span of the approach ledge. A portal in its center is just large enough to allow one person at a time to squeeze slowly through, necessarily head first. A lone sentry stationed out there—man, woman, or older child—armed with stone club, spear, or atlatl (a cleverly engineered, arm-powered dart launcher that predated the bow and arrow by millennia in the Americas), could hold back a small army of invaders as they attempted, one doomed fool at a time, to penetrate the defensive wall.

Like the overwhelming majority of Anasazi cliff dwellings everywhere—at least at such small, isolated sites as here—this place was chosen not only for its proximity to farmland but for its defensibility. Obviously this was a hidden family fortress built in dire fear of ancient enemies: Transient raiders up from Old Mexico? Internecine rivals from neighboring Anasazi clans? Roving bands of outlaw outcasts? I go with the latter.

By the time this stone retreat was built, the Anasazi, having been in residence hereabouts for centuries, had enjoyed so much growth and progress they'd all but grown and progressed themselves right out of business. Entire forests had been clear-cut (the hard way, with stone axes) for timber and fuel, wildlife had been extirpated by overhunting, wild plants likewise had been too long overharvested, the sparse dry soil unrelentingly overfarmed. In short (the old familiar story of civilization), the human population—thought to have been even larger throughout the Four Corners region then than now—had swelled far beyond the carrying capacity of the local ecology, with no thought given to sustainable resource conservation. Then came the ecological and cultural coup de grace of prolonged drought.

It was during those starving, predictably anarchic last years—during the time this little enclave was built and occupied—that the Anasazi's once-magnificent cultural, trade, and spiritual center at Chaco Canyon, in nearby New Mexico, collapsed (socially and economically if not physically) and was abandoned. Simultaneously and ubiquitously throughout the Four Corners region, unknown raiders, quite likely young male Anasazi renegades, murdered, butchered, cooked, and consumed entire "pre-Puebloan" families. This is no mere macabre speculation: Such gruesome slaughter sites have been scientifically documented throughout Anasazi country, like it or not (and a lot of PC archaeologists openly do not).

Why? My vote goes to social turmoil arising from nutritional stress borne from overpopulation, environmental depletion, and extended drought. In today's New West, "Grow or die" is an economic rallying cry, sounded from small-town chambers of commerce and heard all the way to the nation's capitol. But for the Anasazi—as it has been and will be for countless others—it was not in fact grow *or* die, but grow *and* die.

I stoop low and crawl into one of the four almost identical, low-roofed sleeping rooms—rectangular, just large enough to accommodate a couple of small adults (the Anasazi, like many ancient agriculturists, were not large people) and a child or two. While I can sit comfortably, standing is impossible; the roof, which consists of nothing more than the sloping alcove ceiling, is that low. A single small door/window looks west across the canyon. Smoke-blackened inner walls and ceiling testify that this tiny rock cell was used as a living space. Wooden pegs inserted at even intervals jut from the crumbling mud-plaster of the inner front wall—pegs from which, perhaps, hung buckskin bags and woven-fiber baskets containing valued personal belongings, talismans and magic. Or maybe the precisely leveled line of pegs supported a narrow shelf. Given the extreme confines of space, most likely it was both.

Finished with my inspection of the aboveground dwelling

and storage structures, I walk out toward the edge of the narrow alcove ledge and seat myself at the center of a sunken bowl of earth encircled by a tumbled wall of sandstone blocks. Beneath me (I know from having seen many such places, both before and after excavation) lies a collapsed kiva, or underground ceremonial chamber. In this little pueblo's heyday, down in this dark smoky cellar, the men of the clan would have gathered to talk, sing, smoke, and perform clandestine ceremonies. We can surmise this invisible social history with some confidence, since even today the Pueblo peoples of New Mexico and Arizona—direct descendants of the Anasazi—continue to practice similar, perhaps identical, rites in near-identical kivas.

Seduced by the haunting atmosphere of this place, I consider spending the night—to do so would be, well, an *experience*—but quickly think better of it. There is no firewood. I have little food and insufficient water. The powdered sandstone dust is pervasive and annoying. Besides, respect demands leaving these musty old ruins to the juniper-scented ghosts of the people who, one tearful day, just up and walked away from it all—all that labor, all that security, all that personal and multigenerational clan history—deserting not just this one dwelling but an entire native homeland considered for centuries to be Sipapu—the sacred womb of humanity.

Bottom line, all mystery and speculation aside, the Anasazi are gone. And glancing at the sun, I reluctantly acknowledge that I too must go.

After brushing out my tracks in the dust of the alcove floor, I hug back along the narrow cliff-side trail to the crumbled defensive wall, ease over and scramble back across the slickrock face, up the talus obstacle course, squeezing through the cleft to emerge once again on the sun-bathed canyon rim. In no particular hurry now, I opt to take the scenic route back to camp. After all, out here on the Mesa—in this magical mindscape of petrified waves, perfumed air, and frozen time—*every* route is the scenic route.

a ghost in the night

Exhausted from the day's explorations, I sag into camp at dusk, drop my pack, and slump down to the living heart of this particular Cedar Mesa oasis—a drip-spring tucked away in a shaded slickrock grotto at the head of a small side canyon. Uncapping my two canteens, I place them on the sand beneath twin slow trickles of sparkling water droplets emerging, as if by magic, from a seam in the sandstone wall. There is no sweeter music, wrote Ed Abbey, than the *tink-tink-tink* of desert water dripping into a tin cup—or, in this instance, into aluminum canteens. And there is no sweeter taste, I would add, than cool spring water and a splash of good bourbon whiskey spiced by the tangy smoke of a piñon/juniper campfire in the American Southwest on a gentle spring night such as this one promises to be.

As the day dims and the drip-spring drips, drips, in no hurry whatsoever to satisfy my raging thirst, I stand staring in wonder at this blessed anomaly. Here, as in uncounted similar oases flung by geologic happenstance all across the sun-parched Colorado Plateau, appear fecund riparian plant communities utterly dependent for their survival on scant water emerging improbably—one glimmering droplet at a time—from solid rock. Like the biblical burning bush, desert drip-springs are miracles in the wilderness—miracles you can *drink*.

Here, as in so many canyon-country elsewhere, enlivening the damp grotto wall along and below the horizontal seep-line are lush green folds of moss. Directly below, in and around the pellucid little pool, thrives a refreshing desert garden of cattails, bracken ferns, Indian rice grass and one saucy, red-lipped, perplexingly named, unbearably beautiful monkey flower (*Mimulus eastwoodiae*).

At my feet (blessedly bare of boots again), the damp sand rimming the pool provides a guest register of recent visitation. From the clear fresh prints I read that a cottontail rabbit, various tiny rodents, a fox, and an adult mule deer, the usual lot of thirsty desert mammals, have been here recently.

Nor—by George!—is that all.

Nearby, in the grotto's slickrock bottom, in the failing light, at the periphery of my vision, at a place where rainwater runoff has washed a few inches of sand into a depression and left it damp, I discern an odd imprint, eerily familiar yet enigmatic. After fumbling in a pocket for my miniflashlight, I move closer to investigate. There, the pale yellow beam cuts through the graying twilight gloom to reveal a track as big as a big man's palm—much larger than any coyote, though not so big as an adult bear—and no claw marks. The bi-lobed front edge and tri-lobed rear of the wide palm pad are clearly distinguished in the impressionable sand and irrefutably indicative of . . . cougar. The single print is sharp-edged, moist, chillingly fresh. I search all around but find no others. Apparently, the big cat ventured just this one step off the slickrock toward the spring, then inexplicably withdrew.

My skin prickles with the knowledge that one of the most sublime megapredators in North America has been here, *right here,* and not so long ago—a beast of the elite clan popularly, and rightly, referred to as "charismatic megafauna."

Back at the track, I drop to my knees and study the print from every angle, then stand again and point the little flashlight all around. But the batteries are weak, and the limping beam is all but useless. Too soon, both twilight and flashlight will fade completely, and I'll be left here in the dark (as my father liked to say) "like Moses when the lights went out." And utterly alone—or, more worrisome yet, *not* alone. A tingle crawls up my spine and I feel my pulse accelerate.

Be cool, I counsel myself. Like the old saw says, there's nothing to fear but . . . what? Why is it we tend to fear the unseen more than the visible, the unknown more than the known, the uncertain more than the absolute?

Mountain lion

Statistically, you are several hundred times less likely to be attacked by a mountain lion than to be struck by lightning. Yet, *you* aren't here, *I* am. There isn't a storm cloud in sight and statistics don't count for shit when the biggest lion track I've ever seen is fresh at my feet and my heart is hammering in my throat.

Wasting time no more, I snatch up the two sloshing, half-filled canteens in one hand—the quart they hold between them will have to do until morning—clutch the increasingly impotent flashlight in the other hand, and scurry back to nearby camp and the comforts of home and hearth. While it's only a couple of hundred yards from the spring, camp is up and out of the darkling grotto and in the relative open and thus, perhaps falsely, reassuring.

After replacing the spent flashlight batteries with spares from my pack, I distract myself with evening chores: retrieve ground cloth, sleeping pad, and bag from the piñon in which they've hung all day to freshen in the fragrant shade; arrange them neatly on the soft sand—a bit nearer the fire than last night; kindle a companionable blaze; boil water for tea; then scorch and devour a big bloody elk steak brought from home—still frozen yesterday but way past thawed tonight. We sure don't need any lion bait lying about.

Much later, following the usual flame-gazing, whisky-sipping, and internal campfire philosophizing, I toss a final club of wood atop the shimmering pool of red-orange coals, then strip and slide into the cocoonish comfort of my sleeping bag. Just me, ten thousand desert stars above (the most, I read somewhere, the unaided human eye can discern), and two butterfly-sized bats—Mexican free-tails, I presume—flitting and diving amongst the confused multitude of moths circling the fading edges of firelight.

Unavoidably, my mind keeps traveling back to that big round track down by the spring, and sleep is a long time coming.

Around midnight, my fitful sleep is happily interrupted by a family of coyotes, yammering maniacally, sounding (I know from long experience) much closer and more numerous than they are. How I love that wild, uncensored music! That anthem of freedom, self-reliance, and joy!

The fire, once so warm and cheering, has grown cold as worn-out love. I manage to hold my eyes open just long enough to witness one green-tailed shooting star making an ambitious rush for the western horizon, only, like so many human dreamers, to burn out and die in the trying.

Some time later, when the dream comes, it is shapeless, blind, and haunting. There are no visual images but only eerie, suspiring, susurrus sounds—like the guarded footfalls of a prowler, breathing shallow and fast. Feeling vaguely threatened by this spooky chimera, I come wide awake and rise on my elbows. Though I'm warm in my bag, my arms are pimpled with gooseflesh. I peer into the swampy darkness but see only black. I listen, but no sound comes. All is quiet in the anthracite desert night. The stars have dimmed, the coyotes gone quiet, even the owls and crickets have hushed, predicting incipient dawn. I consider switching on the flashlight for a good look around, but don't, for fear I'll think myself a coward come morning.

Finally, feeling foolish, reminding myself it was only a dream, I lie back and hope for sleep to return.

In the amber glow of morning, I wake bleary-eyed and groggy to discover that the night's eerie dream was no dream at all. There, in the powdery sand just a body's length out from my sleeping place and imprinted over one of my own bare footprints, is a big round track.

I unzip my bag, struggle out, stand and peer around. The prints are everywhere. Over there, the lion approached from the sage. And those odd marks show where he, or she, sat back on bony haunches, long tail sweeping an arc in the desert dust. From that reflective repose I imagine the prowler staring at me with huge nocturnal eyes, listening, sniffing my acrid, sweaty scent, panting softly, pondering the innocent sleeper in inscrutable feline fashion.

As best I can read the jumbled sign, it appears the cat then moved to the far side of the fire pit and haunch-sat again. And over there, its curiosity apparently satisfied—or maybe I startled it with my sudden awakening—the spectral visitor padded back into the sage from which it had come. Perhaps it remains nearby even now, watching and waiting, biding its time, biding mine.

Succumbing to a reckless urge, I pull on shorts, lace boots over sockless feet, and follow the departing trail. But the prints soon strike slickrock. And that is that.

Warmed by strong camp coffee and growing increasingly relaxed under a brilliant morning sun, I sit and reflect. Had the cat been looking to make a meal of me, it likely could have. Pumas are predation perfected, capable of bringing down not just deer, but creatures as large as elk, cattle, even horses—and on very rare occasion, people. Stalking close, then pouncing after a short rush, the cougar kills by sinking long canines into the skull or neck of its startled prey, then clamping, viselike, with powerful jaws while ripping and shredding with the fanglike dewclaws inside both forearms. It's a high-risk way to earn a living—those sharp, flying deer hooves thrashing in your face—and most lions show the scars of their profession. By comparison, a naked snoring man would be cake.

Obviously, predation was not the cat's intent. Or perhaps it was, but drawing near, the keen-nosed animal was offended by my unwashed, unappetizing aroma. But far more likely, I spooked it from the spring last night, and it's been lurking nearby ever since, curious as a cat, innocent of ill intent.

Was I in any danger? I'll never know for sure. And just as well.

Which is to say, with all my introductory carrying on about magic and spirituality, I am not a spiritual person in any mystical, otherworldly sense of the term. Magical thinking of any stripe sends me sprinting for the nearest exit to reality. What I can see, hear, smell, taste, and caress is plenty good enough for me, here and hereafter. Yet, out here in the ancient dust, out here among Anasazi ghosts and nocturnal dream creatures, out here in the pulsing heart of the living Old West—here in this place where spirits dwell—I feel that I've been touched by magic.

PART II The Natural Bridges Story

under the horse's belly

Long after the Anasazi had gone, long before Branson and I arrived, many others passed this way: explorers, adventurers, cowboys, gold and uranium prospectors, mapmakers, Mormon settlers, merchants, and hardy horseback tourists. While few stayed on, the legacies of their passing heavily invest Cedar Mesa today. This is one such legacy:

On a late summer day in 1883, a balding, massively mustachioed prospector named Cass Hite, in company with three companions, rode southeast from their placer-mining camp on the Colorado River and into the sandstone mouth of White Canyon. Guiding the three white gold diggers was a Paiute man known to history only as Indian Joe. While nothing suggests that Hite set out with foreknowledge and intent to find the world's greatest assemblage of natural stone bridges, it's likely that Indian Joe had told him of them, sparking his interest. For countless generations, the Paiute people had known of, visited, and mythologized the great rock spans, referring to them by the poetically descriptive term *Mah-vah-talk-tump,* "Under the Horse's Belly." No matter though, for the European-derived rule of discovery is this: The first white guy to spread the news to the white world gets the history-book credit.

Fortunately, Hite's dismally banal names for these awesome natural wonders — President, Senator, and Congressman — failed to take root in the public or even the political imagination, and soon were replaced by the lyrical and vastly more apropos Hopi honorifics Sipapu, Kachina, and Owachomo. In his 1908 field notes, government surveyor William B. Douglas explains why he assigned these names:

> A conspicuous feature of the little bridge is a conical mound, on top of, and forming a part of the bridge rock [suggesting] the name of "Owachomo" (Rock Mound) Bridge, a name in actual use by the Hopi. The middle bridge is in reality named by the symbols carved on it, requiring only an interpretation. Of these is the Lightning Snake, a symbol which was painted on the bodies of the Kachina (the Sacred Dancers). . . . The White Canyon bridge, the largest and most impressive of the three, forms a great portal across the canyon through which all who follow the canyon trail must pass [suggesting] the Sipapu, which according to the cosmogonic mythology of the Hopi and kindred tribes, is the gate-

Sipapu Bridge, Natural Bridges National Monument

way through which man comes to life from the underworld, and through which he must finally depart.

Douglas had come to chart this remote rock desert because, shortly before, President Theodore Roosevelt—America's most forceful and effective champion of wildlands conservation—had employed the American Antiquities Act to protect the three bridges and their surrounds as Utah's first national monument.

And that's how Natural Bridges National Monument came to be a national monument. How the bridges themselves came to be, and when, are far more compelling mysteries.

Like the story of life itself, the Natural Bridges saga opens in the shallow seas of antiquity. During the Permian geological period, some 260 million years ago, a great inland sea inundated much of what we know today as the American West. Along the eastern shoreline of this sea, beach sand blew this way and that, layer upon layer, marking the changing winds of time. Simultaneously, sea-floor sand remained in a state of constant agitation, rippled and layered endlessly by shifting currents.

Across the eons, as the land slowly rose and the sea dried up, those wind- and water-sculpted sands hardened to form today's multilayered, cross-bedded Cedar Mesa sandstone. It is this formation, in places 1,200 feet thick, from which the three great bridges were sculpted. By around 10 million years ago, the inland sea was ancient history, leaving the Colorado Plateau high and dry. In its place, flowing sluggishly across this vast, relatively flat surface, were the ancestral Colorado River and its tributaries. The heavy loads of grit suspended in these streams ground lazy, meandering channels into the underlying sandstone, patiently excavating White and Armstrong canyons. Erosion never sleeps, and at each horseshoe bend in the two canyons' meandering streams, as the water bore ever deeper into the plateau, isolated walls of standing stone took shape. Over time, the endless onslaught of water honed these isolated walls ever thinner, reducing them finally to the slender upright features we know today as fins. (For a world-class display of natural stone fins, visit Arches National Park.)

And so it went. When the streams ran low and slow, which they mostly did, nothing happened fast. But with each flash flood, a common occurrence in desert country, the roaring torrent of floodwater, with its multiton cargo of tumbling rocks and uprooted trees, battered calamitously against the upstream face of each increasingly delicate fin. Eventually, the floods punched completely through the bases of some fins—straightening the streams, bypassing the meanders, and forming infant bridges. Beyond this point, with water now running *through* the fins, the bridges grew much faster.

Aiding hydraulic erosion—nature's primary bridgemaker—was the relentless conspiracy of gravity and the alternate freezing and thawing, expanding and shrinking, of moisture trapped in the porous stone, precipitating the spalling, or breaking away, of sometimes massive slabs from the undersides of each bridge. Windblown grit helped to polish and finish the job. (In fact and of course, the insidious workings of time and geology are never finished. As recently as June, 1992, Kachina spalled a 4,000-ton pebble from its belly—*not* a good day to have been relaxing there-under in the shade, as Branson and I had done just a few weeks before.)

In summary review: A natural bridge is bored through a sandstone fin by running water and always spans an active or former stream. Far more common than bridges, however, are natural arches, another species of large hole eroded through a fin. But an arch has no stream beneath it. Rather, an arch is carved by the freezing and thawing of groundwater pooled in cracks and pockets. As this liquid lever freezes and expands, it doggedly widens the cracks and weakens the surrounding stone, precipitating spalling. Gravity and wind aid the effort, but not running water.

Last and least, a small, adolescent arch with a considerable mass of rock all around is a *window*.

the human history of natural bridges

As was the case throughout prehistoric America, geology dictated locally adaptive forms of human economy, spirituality, architecture and art.

In yet another geologic phenomenon unique to Utah canyon country, the vertical faces of many sandstone cliffs became coated with a black, shiny, mineralized patina called desert varnish. It was into this dark backdrop that Anasazi artists pecked their eerie petroglyphs. At the same time, on the lighter surfaces of unvarnished Cedar Mesa sandstone—beige to white—these same primitive surrealists created colorful paintings called *pictographs.*

In addition to the "lightning snakes" noted by William Douglas, Anasazi rock art features abundant images of desert bighorn sheep and other animals and their tracks, plus wildly abstract geometric and spherical designs, and even human handprints. The latter were commonly rendered by pressing the artist's (or a model's) hand hard against a sandstone wall, fingers spread, then mouth-blowing powdered or liquefied pigment around the flesh-and-bone stencil to form an outline image. Another approach was to dip a hand or foot into the pigment and make a direct-pressure application. But far and away the most compelling of Anasazi art themes are the ghostly, always behorned, humanoid figures called anthropomorphs. Overtly magical in both appearance and meaning, these not-uncommon Anasazi spooks lend much to the undeniable ethereal ambiance of Natural Bridges National Monument and all of Cedar Mesa.

Yet while the Anasazi are today the most archaeologically and historically visible of prehistoric Cedar Mesa visitors, they were hardly the first.

Millennia before the Anasazi arrived at Cedar Mesa, mysterious peoples known collectively as Paleo-Indians visited and repeatedly, if always only briefly, occupied the area. These wandering hunter/gatherers neither erected lasting shelters nor made pottery, thus left little evidence of their nomadic comings and goings. And come and go they did, as the Bridges area was not, as it is not today, an all-season meteorological paradise. In summer, temperatures frequently surpass 100 degrees Fahrenheit. In winter, the canyons of Cedar Mesa, including White and Armstrong, remain shaded and frozen for weeks on end, and snow is not uncommon.

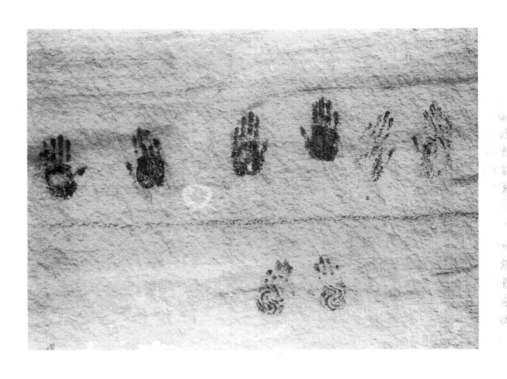

Anasazi rock art in Natural Bridges National Monument

(Additionally today, springtime can bring unbearable swarms of biting gnats, though it's likely these hellish pests did not exist here before the advent of intense livestock grazing and the extensive ecological damage it has wrought.)

Thanks to the Mesa's seasonal harshness, even the increasingly agricultural Anasazi (who existed as an intact culture roughly 1–1300 A.D.) likely remained seminomadic, moving from higher ground to lower in seasonal rounds, as dictated by weather, agricultural needs, wild plant progression, and wildlife movements. But compared to their Paleo precursors' shadowy traces, Anasazi artifacts are bountiful at Bridges. In addition to the aforementioned glyphs and pictos, we find elegant painted pottery; stone, bone (including antler), and wood tools and weapons; and an abundance of masonry structures.

Within the monument, prominent Anasazi structural ruins include small, mesa-top pueblos (Road Loop Ruins), gravity-defying cliff dwellings, and canyon-bottom ruins ranging from kivas (at least one of which I've explored, off the beaten path, is anomalously rectangular, rather than the standard round) to uncharacteristically ornate crypts of unknown purpose (the namesake structures of Horsecollar Ruins).

Yet despite all the cultural litter the Anasazi left behind, the Natural Bridges area was never likely populated by more than a few small extended-family groups at any time. And by 1250 A.D. the last of them were gone, having joined the massive and ultimately complete (by 1300) Anasazi exodus from their increasingly untenable ancestral homeland, seeking (and finding) friendlier country and social conditions among their pre-Hopi kin, far to the south and east.

After the Anasazi's abandonment of the area and for an unknown interval, the three natural bridges saw only sporadic visitors, all of them Indian: the Paiute ancestors of Indian Joe, far-ranging Ute hunting and war parties, Navajo herders and other native wanderers. Then, as we have seen, came the whites—explorers, prospectors, settlers, and monument makers—and all was changed forever.

you and natural bridges

In the early years of tourism in the harsh and sparsely settled American West, visitors to Natural Bridges endured a long train ride to Thompson's Spring, then a thirty-five-mile stagecoach bounce south to Moab, followed by another sixty miles via wagon or horseback to Monticello and a final fifty miles by mule train to Bridges. That's a week of bone-jarring travel across harsh desert terrain (not even counting the train) *just to get there,* where the "touring" finally began.

Today, most visitors to Natural Bridges are of the common subspecies *Homo touron motorensis.* If they debark from their climate-controlled vehicles at all, it's usually only to point a camcorder in a scenic direction from a roadside overlook. For such

Kachina Bridge, Natural Bridges National Monument

fast-food modern tourism, Natural Bridges has been appropriately tamed, with an eight-mile, one-way loop road—Bridge View Drive—leading to roadside overlooks of all three bridges and much scenic more. But for those who want a *lot* scenic more—a memorable movie rather than a mere snapshot—it's easily attainable just a short hike away.

The first bridge along the drive, Sipapu, is the largest in the monument and the second-largest natural bridge in America (narrowly trailing Rainbow Bridge at nearby Lake Powell). Rising 220 feet above the canyon floor, Sipapu spans 268 feet. Kachina is the second bridge along the loop drive and the second-largest in the monument, standing 210 feet high with a span of 204 feet. Finally, Owachomo, the "little bridge," is a "mere" 106 feet high and spans "only" 180 feet (hardly worth mentioning, eh?).

Each of the three bridges is accessible by a well-marked, lizard-infested foot trail. In places, these paths can be challenging, even modestly exciting, but never really dangerous for anyone blessed with good health, normal balance, and common survival sense. One-way distances range from a minimum of .2 miles (Owachomo) to a maximum of .75 miles (Kachina). Elevation loss (thus, return-trip climb) varies from 180 feet (Owachomo) to 500 feet (Sipapu).

Of those three strolls, I predict you'll find Sipapu the most rewarding. On your way down (.6 miles), you'll negotiate two long, cliff-hanging flights of metal stairs, a modestly narrow cliff-side trail shaded by a shallow alcove, some moderately steep slickrock stretches, and, if you so choose, a short spur trail leading to a small Anasazi ruin perched above a rounded slickrock face without guardrail, from which it would be as easy as "Oops!" to fall, jump, or be pushed. Especially when it's wet or icy.

The view from this aerie, at the vertiginous terminus of the Sipapu spur trail, is unparalleled in the developed realm of the monument and a world-class rush if you (like Branson) are into high-octane adrenaline pumps. Still at the end of the spur trail, if you're carrying binoculars, search the far facing cliff wall for the most inaccessible Anasazi cliff dwellings imaginable. Not even a helicopter and rappelling rig could get you into there— but only, perhaps, being shot from a cannon.

How, then, did the "primitive" Anasazi do it? Branson, in line with common archaeological consensus, used to argue for long ladders, long ropes, and courage hard as stone—until he went out to dinner (once) with a young lady from Sedona, Arizona, who claimed in all seriousness to be from the Pleiades and to have certain knowledge of "where the Anasazi disappeared to." Where? Branson asked, imitating the gentleman he in fact always is. "They're up *there* [she pointed reverently skyward], orbiting Earth in space ships, watching over us, awaiting the right time to return and teach us how to live in peace." And so it all comes clear! With technology like *that,* cliff-dwelling access for the Anasazi would have been just a beam-up away.

From the base of Sipapu, an additional down-canyon jaunt of a mile or so leads to Horsecollar Ruins. This charming Anasazi site in the accessible monument comprises a beautifully preserved (though roofless) kiva and two small, conical structures named for the horsecollar shapes of their doorways. Too small to live in (though both have seen fires), and too ornate to be mill-run storage bins . . . what might have been their purpose? Yet another unsolved mystery, delicious as fresh-baked bread.

For most visitors, the ultimate Natural Bridges hiking experience is an eight-mile canyon-bottom meander from Sipapu to Owachomo, passing beneath Kachina about midway. Only trouble with this little adventure is that due to the one-way road, you'll need two vehicles for a shuttle. Otherwise, one of your party (most effectively, she or he wearing the least filth and body odor) will have to hitchhike around the loop and back to your wheels, then return to fetch the survivors. Given the continual flow of traffic, it's generally a snap. (However, since regulations can change, check with a ranger before extending your thumb.)

With the White Canyon hike under your boots and in your heart, you're ready to move beyond the buzzing bounds of the monument, away from the motorized crowds, off the beaten path . . . out there on your own.

PART III   Down in the Canyons

raid at Comb Wash, redux

*O*ne fine day in early June, bearing west from Blanding, Utah . . . the gang paused at the summit of Comb Ridge for a look at the world below. . . . Comb Ridge is a great monocline, rising gradually on the east side, dropping off at an angle close to ninety degrees on the west side. The drop-off from the rim is about five hundred feet straight down, with another three hundred feet or more of steeply sloping talus below the cliff. Like many other canyons, mesas, and monoclines in southeast Utah, Comb Ridge forms a serious barrier to east-west land travel. Or it used to. God meant it to.

— Edward Abbey, "The Raid at Comb Wash," from *The Monkey Wrench Gang*

Comb Ridge

One fine day in early April, Branson and I descend into Owl Creek Canyon, just west of the massively serrate cliffs of Comb Ridge and its namesake wash to the west below. Owl is one of five primary sandstone clefts drained by Comb Wash—the others being Arch, Mule, Road, and Fish Creek. All are rugged, remote, and sublime.

Like Shakespeare's *Richard II,* down, down we go. But unlike that dead guy, Branson and I are not descending a throne in defeat. We are descending into a throne room of natural wildness to celebrate life.

The Owl Creek trailhead, like so much of Cedar Mesa, is set in a sea of lapping slickrock, framed by some of the Four Corners' most prominent landmarks. To the north, just east of Natural Bridges, protrude the near-twin buttes (flat-topped mountains) called, poetically apropos, the Bear's Ears. Northeastward rise the Abajo Mountains, one of several isolated "island" ranges hereabouts, and the Abajos' lofty peninsula, Elk Ridge. Off in the southeast, overlooking the homeland of the Mountain Ute Indian Tribe, Ute Mountain—better known locally as the Sleeping Ute, which it rather resembles when viewed from east or west—snores eternally. Meanwhile, low and dark on the afternoon horizon, sacred to the indigenous Navajo and much-tortured by profiteers, Black Mesa broods.

It's beyond beautiful in every direction from here, and the on-trail hiking is easy—until you come, soon and suddenly, to the brink of the world and begin the rocky plunge to the canyon floor hundreds of feet below.

The descent to Owl Creek is merely interesting for moderately experienced and unburdened canyon-country hikers. But strap a motel on your back and all is changed—balance and footing become critical. Your first misstep could be your last. Slowly and gingerly, therefore—scuttling over boulders, crouching under limby piñon and juniper, creeping across dangerously exposed slickrock slopes—you pick and shuffle your careful way down.

Long before you reach the bottom, you spot a small prehistoric ruin perched on the west canyon wall. Ignore this minor structure and continue on—down, down—to a far more impressive ruin set back in a lovely alcove directly below the canyon's head (and thus, easily accessible to day hikers). This time you stop, drop your pack on the trail, hop off a low ledge, and do the dusty detour. Your reward is a well-preserved, aboveground kiva. Most kivas, as we've seen, are subterranean. But where solid rock flooring prevents digging, as with the example at hand—well, necessity is the mother of compromise.

The Owl Creek kiva's roof—a multiple layer-cake of beams, lattice, juniper bark, and adobe (in all, it resembles proto "Santa Fe style")—was long ago pulled off by looters. But the walls, though fragile and apt to collapse the next time some monkey-brained muttonhead tries to scale them, remain for now intact. Inspect the raggedy ends of the roof beams lying scattered about, and you'll see the beaver-bite marks of stone axes that were manufactured, employed, and abandoned some half a millennium before that infamous troublemaker Columbus was even born.

Behind the kiva squat three smaller structures, also of stone and adobe, in the customary storage-bin guise of giant beehives. (Whether coincidental or ironical, Utah today bills itself as "the beehive state.") Capping the top hatch to one of the bins is a thin, hand-shaped slab of sandstone, fragile as glass. The sense of another time, another world, another worldview, is palpable and a little spooky. You can almost hear old Kokopelli, the hunch-backed backdoor man of Anasazi art and legend, icon of fertility, tooting his flute, beckoning the girls to come out and play while the boys are away. (The original "traveling salesman and the farmer's wife" story.)

The first time Branson brought me here, many years ago, it was winter and snow was falling in huge wobbly flakes, like leaves from autumn aspens, lending a quiet surrealism to the view beyond the alcove roof and down the red-and-white-striped sandstone abyss. Today is likewise stormy, if not so brisk. Virgas, dark curtains of falling water that promise hope but evaporate before reaching the parched ground, streak the southern horizon. The desert smells like rain.

Tempting as it is to dally in this place of lingering spirits, we got a late start, it's late afternoon already, and the troubled, churning heavens impart in me if not in the ever-calm Branson a sense of urgency to find a good campsite and get settled in. Having touched nothing and leaving not even tracks in the ancient dust, we return to our packs, saddle up, and carry on.

Within the hour the gloom has lifted.

The sun stood high in the clouds; the air was still and warm.

From far below rises the sparkling voice of a canyon wren, each note more precious than a diamond. For those who know and love Utah canyon country, the pellucid voice of *Catherpes mexicanus* is more than a joy to hear; it's a natural blessing, a desert benediction. What the loon gives to the northern lake country, the canyon wren gives alike to southwestern canyon country. And that "what" is musical magic.

We complete the descent to the canyon floor without mishap and loaf on down-creek. Only a few miles along, just below the first big pour-off ledge—often, these slickrock canyon streambeds, as they cut through soft sedimentary layers of varying resistance, erode unevenly to form giant stairsteps, some of which are impassable and over which roaring flash floods, indeed, pour off—we come to a campsite too good to pass by. We have three days to enjoy a hike of only twenty miles or so—down Owl to its confluence with Fish Creek Canyon at Comb Wash, up Fish Creek to the climb-out, then a short stroll back to the trailhead—so where's the rush?

Immediately, I dub this place Dragon Tree Amphitheater, in honor of the convoluted cottonwood guarding its entrance. Like everything else in these canyons, the tree is ageless and massive. Its trunk is five feet through and forked near the bottom. One big subtrunk undulates along the ground to frame the cloistered campsite. The other rises above our heads (the dragon's back), then dips sharply (neck) and rises again (head), before drooping and tapering in a long pointy snout. Completing the image, from the dragon's head protrude a pair of woody horns.

We guess the amphitheater to be a hundred yards front to

back, half that wide, and twice as deep (or high, depending on your perspective). Its vertical walls are sculpted from Cedar Mesa sandstone in alternating bands of rose and gray. From the back of the grotto, glinting like quicksilver, beckons a shallow pool. On closer inspection, its water is the color of tea—filter before drinking—supplied by a seep that slithers down a slickrock slot and trickles, tinkling like a hundred crystal chimes, over two stone ledges to the pool, thirty feet below. From sedimentary seams in the walls encircling the pool hang a profusion of columbines, now flowerless in spring green but soon to blossom in flaming red.

The afternoon sun flares blindingly, burns like flame, on the mirrored pool. The drip-fall tinkles hypnotically. Just above the canyon rim one blue-black raven, insignificant against the vast azure sky, babbles incoherently at the universe. Much higher, an anonymous raptor soars in easy arcs.

One thin scream came floating down, like a feather, from the silver-clouded sky . . . solitaire, one hawk passing far above the red reef, above the waves of Triassic sandstone.

Driftwood, replenished by periodic flash floods, is abundant out in the main canyon, and my fuel-collecting circuit takes me there. Looking south, I spot a motley crew of monolithic sandstone hoodoos standing eternal guard over this ancient sacred place—two sphinxes, one potbellied mummy, and an owl as tall as a five-story building.

Stooping for a stick of wood, I almost tromp a stamp-sized

shard of pinched-coil pottery. I inspect the unpainted, utilitarian fragment, wondering at the stories it knows, then return it to its place in time. Happily burdened with firewood, I return campward.

As usual, Branson announces his intent to sleep out tonight. Unswayed by this blatant display of machismo, I pitch my tent—I lugged the bulky bastard down here, I'll lug it back up, and I don't intend to see all that effort go to waste. Besides, who knows when rain might come? With only a few degrees of sky visible between soaring canyon walls, a storm can catch you unawares.

Tent up, I torch my little alcohol stove (just a small metal cup into which you pour an inch or so of fuel, light, then sit your pot on top: slow but lightweight and compact, cheap, and most important in my case, foolproof). When the water hits a boil, I'll rehydrate the green-colored veggie gravel that will have to do us for dinner.

Branson, meanwhile, busies himself cleaning out and rebuilding the circular stone fire ring.

The previous campers left not a tatter of litter, bless them, but ignorantly filled the hearth with rocks and sand. A wilderness no-no, this, since the next tenants, rather than cleaning out the sooty pit, will likely construct a whole new ring—only to fill *it* in when they leave. In no time, after this thoughtless fashion, hearths and ashes are everywhere and another pristine campsite is ruined. (Note: Shortly after the expedition chronicled here, this became such a problem, together with the depletion of deadwood in the canyon bottoms, that campfires in all primary Comb Wash canyons were banned. So it goes.)

Blessed evening at last.

Now the stillness was complete. The watchers . . . eating their suppers from tin plates, heard the croon of a mourning dove far down the wash. . . . The great golden light of the setting sun streamed across the sky, glowing upon the clouds and the mountains. Almost all the country within their view was roadless, uninhabited, a wilderness. They meant to keep it that way.

At dusk Branson and I are treated to a private rock concert when a canyon wren invades the amphitheater and commences singing his (or her) pointy little head off, the fluted serenade enhanced to choirlike proportions by the superb echo acoustics of this stony place.

Come full darkness and the wren falls quiet, or leaves unseen, only to be replaced by a duo of base-voiced frogs in the pool at the back of the grotto. From the sound of them, it's a mating pair.

"*Come-ere.*"

"*No way.*"

"*Come-ere!*"

"*Okay!*"

The frolicking frogs prove to be real party animals, croaking late into the night. The wind rises sporadically, blowing sand and big dollops of rain against my nylon abode. Too far off to hear its thunder, heat lightning strobes, like battling sky gods of Grecian myth. I toss restlessly through it all, while out there on his beloved dirt, rolled up in a tarp, the unflappable Branson (all six-foot-three of him) snores blissfully on.

The dawn sky is clean and filled with promise, prompting us to hit the trail at the crack of . . . midmorning. I use the term "trail" here loosely, recalling with a chuckle a comment scribbled by a returned hiker in the trailhead register:

"More signs, please!"

In fact, even one sign would be one more than we've seen so far—and one too many. If you want signs, hike in a national park or on any popular Forest Service trail. Cedar Mesa is a place for adventure. For getting lost and finding your own way out (or not). For following footprints in the sand and pebble cairns across long stretches of undifferentiated slickrock. For self-discovery. I thank the canyon gods that the BLM doesn't share the Forest and Park services' compulsion (or, more likely, their budgets) for pampering a dilettante public and insulting the scenery with "More signs, please!"

As we walk, Branson and I play Name That Flora. We're a month too early for the best of it—precious few flowers have bloomed just yet, the cottonwoods have barely begun to unfurl their lime-green leaves, and by and large the wilted browns of winter still dominate. Even so, we have the ubiquitous verdure of the P-J on the mesa tops above, plus down here Mormon tea, buffalo berry, yuccalike nests of deadly green spears, an occasional sanguine bouquet of Indian paintbrush, a few lavender vetch, some homely locoweed, and several unknown varieties of LYFs (little yellow flowers).

In places along the creek we wade through thickets of cattails and *Equisetum*. The latter—a reed commonly called horsetail joint grass—erupts here (and there) thick as a shaggy dog's hair and higher than our heads, creating an atmosphere more evocative of a Southeast Asian jungle than the desert Southwest.

We approach another pour-off. Below its abrupt ledge lies what Branson, who's been here often before, calls Deep Pool. Here the little creek plunges thirty feet to a pond I guess to be twenty yards across and appearing, indeed, so very deep it's hard even to imagine a bottom. What mysteries lie in those hazy depths?

"I dove down deep as I could one time," Branson tells me, "went halfway to China but couldn't find the bottom."

Here, as at Dragon Tree, the walls encircling the pool drip green with leafing, as-yet-flowerless columbines. Yard-long clumps of dry brown bunchgrass hang inverted from the rusty cliffs and bright new dandelions enliven the narrow beach. Also on that beach, a pair of slate-gray dippers (water ouzels) perform their dips (like feathered lizards doing push-ups), then take wing and away, chirruping gaily.

We work our way up along a side ledge then drop down below the pool to an oasis of cottonwoods, bare now but on the verge of shading another idyllic campsite. Only thing missing from this picture, observes my career bachelor friend, is a bevy of longhaired canyon nymphs, basking naked in the midday sun. As usual, laid-back Branson is in no hurry to leave. ("Who knows when those nymphs might show?") But we got a lazy start, the trail is long ahead, and I am annoyingly persistent.

With another hour and a couple more miles under our boots,

we round a bend and meet, towering to port astern, a *true* Owl Canyon nymph, whom we dub the Cameo Lady: hair pulled back modestly in a Mormon-style bun, eyes coyly closed, face downcast, shy and demure. This, she, the Cameo Lady, is the most realistic natural stone sculpture I've ever seen, shaped and honed by eons of mindless meteorology. She is also our signal to camel-up, says Branson. We're nearing the lower canyon and confluence, and for the next few miles, water is reliably unreliable.

When we come to the next pool, a foot deep and clear, we stop and unsaddle. I fish out my old cheap filter pump from my old cheap backpack, Branson does likewise, and we squat and pump and drink until our tongues float, then pump some more to top our canteens. Finished and moving to stand, I slip on a wet rock and fall butt first into the pool.

Branson smiles but does not laugh, and as I'm changing into dry shorts and socks he spins out a story.

"It was right here," my old friend begins, "where I made my most amazing wildlife observation ever. I was just sitting and looking around, when here comes a tiger swallowtail—the lemon-yellow kind with delicate black pinstriping. As the big butterfly went flitting by, I noticed that right behind it, right on its tail, was a little brown bat, the pair of them flying in perfect formation."

"Wow," I respond, thinking he is finished. "A bat chasing a butterfly, in broad daylight no less. I . . ."

"But there's more," Branson interjects. "A minute later, here they came back. And this time, the butterfly was tailgating the bat!"

Nevill's Arch and hoodoos in Owl Creek Canyon

Believe it or not. Knowing both Branson and the fascinating unpredictability of nature as I do, I do.

In due course we round another bend in the canyon walls and there it is, hard to port—the Owl Creek denouement— a massive rock rainbow called Nevill's Arch. Bridging across a hanging side canyon, it is big enough, seems to me, to fly a small jetliner through (so long as I'm not onboard).

And more. Arrayed along the cliff to the south of the arch is a giant's gallery of sandstone hoodoos: a squatting frog, a Mexican hat, a bearded sheik with turban-wrapped head, and a free-standing phallus that's only half erect but sixty feet tall at that.

We stare a good long while, trying to decide whether or not to be envious, then plod reluctantly on.

"Reluctant" because just below Nevill's Arch the canyon walls retreat, the valley opens and flattens, and the slickrock disappears beneath deep, dusty sand. No water nowhere. We are approaching the confluence—the lowest, hottest, most severely cow-trampled and withal, least enjoyable, leg of the hike.

toward a confluence of views

There's no gain in glossing it over: The Comb Wash confluence of Owl and Fish creek canyons is a dry, shade-starved sagebrush flat bristling with thistle, snakeweed, rabbitbrush, cheatgrass, locoweed, tumbleweed, and other noxious invaders symptomatic of long-term livestock overgrazing. Prickly pear, another invasive species, abounds. The once-and-former stream banks are trampled, eroded, utterly denuded of riparian green-ery, and the channel runs wide and talc-dry. Fine red dust coats our skin and grits in our eyes when we blink.

Even so and happily—in spite of all these ugly symptoms and more of a tragic history of "wise use" abuse by thoughtless

Pool of water in Arch Canyon

ranchers and their lackeys at the local BLM headquarters and in Washington—it's a hell of a lot better here now than it was just a few years ago. And each coming spring will be greener yet because the cows and their keepers have been given the boot.

Likewise with the other primary feeder canyons of Comb Wash: no more cows. At least for now. And best of all, these cowless, healing canyons offer visible, quantifiable proof that concerned, tenacious individuals—the proverbial "little" guys and gals—*can* make a difference. To wit:

Back in March of 1988, just after the winter grazing season, Joseph Feller, a law professor at Arizona State University in Tempe, took a hike in nearby Arch Canyon. What Feller saw there, he told me, was "appalling . . . cow pies everywhere. The vegetation had all been grazed down to root stubble. The stream banks and microbiotic crust were trampled and destroyed. It looked like a war zone." Feller headed home determined to do something about the mess that had spoiled this visit to Cedar Mesa, as it had so many others before.

What he did was appeal BLM's Comb Wash grazing practices to BLM's mother agency, the U.S. Department of Interior. Consequently, an Interior Department administrative law judge directed the area BLM boss to explain and reconsider his cram-the-cows-in grazing strategy. Digging in the heels of his cowboy boots, the BLM manager ignored the court's mandate and issued another grazing permit, without modifications, to the Ute Mountain Ute Indian Tribe. (Indians cum cowboys: the New West.)

No quitter, the tenacious Feller recruited two powerful conservation organizations—the National Wildlife Federation and the Southern Utah Wilderness Alliance—to join him in filing a second, much broader appeal. Meanwhile, rallying behind the BLM were the usual pro-grazing suspects: the American Farm Bureau Federation, the Public Lands Council (a "wise use" group), the National Cattlemen's Association, the American Sheep Industry Association, the Ute Mountain Ute Indian Tribe, et al.

I'd heard through the grapevine what was going on, and had written a few letters on the appellants' behalf. Eventually, I was invited to testify regarding the condition of my favorite Cedar Mesa retreat before and after a recent winter of abusive grazing around the very spring where the nocturnal lion had dropped by to enliven my dreams. The outcome of it all was a rare sweet victory in the battle to return America's public lands to the American public. At its heart, the verdict read: "BLM is hereby prohibited from allowing any grazing in the canyons until an adequate EIS [Environmental Impact Statement] is prepared and considered [and] until BLM makes a reasoned and informed decision that grazing the canyons is in the public interest. . . ."

One brave act is worth a thousand brave words.

Certainly, when I run short on deer and elk meat—*real* meat, the healthy, low-fat sort that human omnivores evolved to eat— I love a thick pink beefsteak as much as the next cholesterol junkie. But the western public lands produce an insignificant 2

Microbiotic crust

percent of the red meat consumed in the United States annually, at an unconscionable cost to the local ecology and economy, to recreation, and to peace in the valley. Rather than the traditional lack of compromise between abusers and preservers of our precious public lands, an amiable confluence of views, benefiting both sides as well as the land, would be a refreshing change.

And so it is, as we round the bend and head up the dusty dry bed of Fish Creek, Branson and I tally the evidence of natural resurrection since the cowboys were cowed. What few beef-plops remain are so desiccated by now that they no longer smell, squish underfoot, or attract the flies that for decades made this place a hiker's hell. (Cow-pie fly: the official bird of the "wise use" movement.) Native grasses are fighting their way back, as are wildflowers and other indigenous forbs.

Consequently, with more and better food gradually becoming available, and without having to compete with cows, wildlife is also returning. As we walk, we count the prints of deer, coyotes, rabbits, lizards, ring-tailed cats, and more. In places, even the microbiotic crust is rejuvenating.

Lunch break. While we're chowing, a breeze puffs up, stiffens, and the sky grays over—grayest in the north, of course, the way we are headed.

After a few minutes, rested and restored, we rise and continue up Fish Creek. Long before our water runs dry we come upon a large shallow pool, surrounded by cattails and other riparian vegetation, from which two gorgeous green-heads rise and flap away, quacking their umbrage at our intrusion.

Onward.

More pools, then a living creek, and soon we come to the first in an emerald chain of beaver ponds, a welcome anomaly, you could even say a miracle, in this dehydrated desert place. In the shallow depths of these natural reservoirs lurk the fish for which this creek was named, mere minnowy little suckers and shiners, but fish nonetheless.

Gradually, the breeze becomes a headwind. The sky grows darker. We bull ahead, but soon are forced to seek refuge from twenty knots of blowing sand and raindrops hard as hail. Our emergency port in this sudden storm is a huge isolated boulder with one side deeply undercut by erosion to form a shallow alcove. Atop this giant pebble—fifteen feet above the canyon floor—rests the sun-bleached corpse of a mature cottonwood . . . flash flood? If so, we agree, we would not have wanted to be here to see it. The boulder alcove keeps the rain out, but not the blowing sand. True grit.

When the worst of the storm moves on, so do we.

In late afternoon we encounter the first fellow humanoids we've seen in three days, a boisterous gaggle consisting of two middle-aged men and a dozen teen-aged boys—headed (we give silent thanks) the other way. As we pass and mumble mutual hellos, I notice the boys looking at Branson kind of funnylike and snickering. One precocious prepubic brat grins luridly and winks at my pal. Confused and curious, I turn to my companion of so many years and adventures and for the first time notice his "lipstick"—a bright red stain encircling his mouth, residual from the quart of cherry Kool-Aid he swigged with lunch, no doubt. (Branson's a sugar junkie.)

"Hey," I announce to the passing troop, overly loud perhaps, dramatically stepping back, having caught on and bought into the joke, "I'm not with *him*."

The boys laugh and giggle. Their leaders chuckle. I grin devilishly. Branson appears puzzled. We all move on. When we're out of earshot, I reveal the joke to my baffled bud, suggesting that before we return to civilization he might wash his face.

"Maybe," says B, trying to gain the upper hand. But too late. He is, for the duration of this trip at least, Lipstick Man.

It's evening when we make camp on a sandy bench above a slender slickrock pool. Come another rain, or worse, another blow, the site offers a small alcove with a stone hearth-ring sheltered beneath.

Evening creeps yellow up the eastern canyon wall. A canyon wren sings on cue. We kindle a fire of juniper and bathe in its tangy stream of smoke. Life, once again, is good.

The evening gave way to night, a dense violet solution of starlight and darkness mixed with energy, each rock and shrub and tree and scarp outlined by an aura of silent radiation.

And a halcyon night she is, the stars as bright as hope, thick and delicious as redeye gravy. Sleep comes fast and stays long.

A clear, cool dawn. We squander a luxurious two hours on breakfast, packing, and general geeking around, loath to leave as this is our last day.

An hour up-canyon, we pause to ponder a panel of pictographs decorating the sandstone wall above a broad shallow alcove to the east—big white paintings on a red rock palette. From left to right I discern a serpent, an inverted letter L, a row of inverted pyramids, a circle of five pyramids all pointed inward toward an invisible central point (like the petals of some magical flower), a letter P, and another pyramid flower.

Well, that massive mural certainly meant something to the ancient artists who painted it. And even though I haven't a clue, it also means something to me.

When the canyon makes a fork, we keep left. Soon we come to yet another inviting campsite, this one balanced above a small, cattail-fringed drip-pool. Here the trail jumps a head-high ledge, demanding the removal of our packs. Lipstick Man limbs up first, I pass up the packs and scramble after.

Now the way levels out, leading to one last, lovely pool, this one bright and alive with early blooming cave primrose (good old *Primula specuicola*). Each delicate lavender flower, I note with a smile of recognition, consists of five triangular petals, their points all facing in. A hummingbird, the first I've seen this spring, goes ringing past between us, an iridescent blur of beauty.

From the primrose pool it's all uphill—in places, almost vertically so—hundreds of feet worth. Twice more we're forced to dump our packs and manhandle them up a difficult ledge, and once a short rope-haul is necessary. This open slickrock "trail" up and out of Fish Creek Canyon, marked only sparsely with little rock cairns, is not merely steep, it's damn hard to follow and not infrequently dangerous.

"More signs, please!" I shout to Branson, laughing (a bit insanely, perhaps) at the ironic joke of it.

At the rim (at last!), breathless from the prolonged burst of physical exertion at the end of a long tiring hike, I tell Lipstick Man that I would never *descend* this route wearing a backpack (thanks to gravitational inertia, down is always trickier than up), though I know that others do it all the time. Branson—a mountain goat reincarnate—says nothing, grinning his bright red grin. Many's the time he's done it before (just last week, in fact), and will do it again without pause. And without me. Certainly, this would be a lovely place and a fitting way to die. It's just that there's more to see and more to do and I ain't quite ready yet.

Sun going down. Time to get out of here.

David Petersen (left) and Branson Reynolds on Muley Point

about the author

David Petersen is the author or editor of twelve books, among them *Writing Naturally; Heartsblood: Hunting, Spirituality, and Wildness in America;* and *Elkheart: A Personal Tribute to Wapiti and Their World*. He is a recipient of the Nike Earthwrite award, "recognizing environmental sensitivity and excellence in outdoor journalism," and other professional honors. For the past twenty-two years he and his wife, Caroline, have lived in a self-built cabin in southwest Colorado, less than a half-day's drive from Cedar Mesa, which they visit often.

about the photographer

For the past quarter-century Branson Reynolds has explored, studied, and photographed the landscapes, ancient ruins, wildlife, and native peoples of the American Southwest. His photographs have illustrated numerous calendars and posters and appeared in such national publications as *Outside, Sierra, Backpacker, Wilderness, Wildlife Conservation,* and *The New York Times.* Additionally, his work has been exhibited in galleries in Santa Fe, San Francisco, Toronto, and his hometown of Durango, Colorado. This is Reynolds's second book in cooperation with his friend and neighbor David Petersen.

Library of Congress Cataloging-in-Publication Data

Petersen, David, 1946–

Cedar Mesa : a place where spirits dwell / text by David Petersen ; photographs by Branson Reynolds.

p. cm. — (Desert places)

ISBN 0-8165-2234-0 (pbk. : acid-free paper)

1. Cedar Mesa (San Juan County, Utah)—Description and travel. 2. Cedar
Mesa (San Juan County, Utah)—Pictorial works. 3. Desert ecology—Utah—
Cedar Mesa (San Juan County) 4. Desert ecology—Utah—Cedar Mesa (San
Juan County)—Pictorial works. I. Reynolds, Branson. II. Title. III. Series.

F832.S4 P47 2002

917.92'59—dc21

2002007838